Upgraded to Chronic

Upgraded to Chronic

Almost Dying Taught Me How to Truly Live

prose and poems by
AMY FIGGS

Cover photo credit: Erica Chambers Photography
www.ericachambers.com
Cover sketch credit: Diane Wood
www.dianewoodart.com

ISBN: 978-1-958150-10-8
Upgraded to Chronic: Almost Dying Taught Me How To Truly Live
Paperpack
January 2023

Subjects:
POETRY / Subjects & Themes / Death, Grief, Loss
BODY, MIND & SPIRIT / Inspiration & Personal Growth
BODY, MIND & SPIRIT / Healing / General

Published by Inner Peace Press
Eau Claire, Wisconsin, USA
www.innerpeacepress.com

To Leo and Zuri, who have survived so much... including me.

Special thanks to my Brain Trust: Carla, Derek, and Diane.

I could not have done this without you.

Table of Contents

Prologue

A very dear friend once told me that I will get to write my book when I feel total ownership of the story. When it all becomes mine and only mine. Well, truth be told, at this very moment, I am in a rent-to-own situation with it. I am about 82% through the lease. I can start packing up the nonessentials but am not going anywhere just yet. Unfortunately this story takes up real estate in my head. So I will begin in the hopes that I will own it outright when the time comes to put an end to it.

I really thought my story was a cancer survival story. It's how it all started. Girls gets cancer, girls beats cancer, girl learns lessons from cancer, girl inspires others. But just when you think cancer is the worst thing that can happen to you, you get proven wrong.

I do have a big story. I am the victim, sometimes. I am the villain others. Sometimes I am both at the same time. There is a lot to tell as I have learned many things. I want to share them because I feel like sharing our stories gives people comfort; it makes them seem connected in an increasingly disconnected world. My life and story are not better or worse than anyone else's. They are just what they are. Take from this book what you will. Read my stories, learn my side. Understand me a bit better and maybe by doing so, you can understand yourself a bit better, too. Because that's what happens when we share our stories. We connect and relate and learn.

How to Read This Book

Just like grief, happiness, and trauma aren't linear, so goes the flow of this book. You can start wherever you like, wherever you are called to start, and learn my story. There are seven chapters; the first chapter (Cancer) starts almost in the middle of the book – the prose stories read to the right and the poems for each chapter theme progress to the left. Thank you for endeavouring to know me, even a little bit.

I Am

the sum of my parts
but I am not the sum
of my traumas

or beginning

or any parts in between

things that happened
events that transpired—

are my story
not my suffering

scars and broken
places in me

are my reinvention
not my ruins

I am not fragile
nor weak

I will not break
easily
.....anymore

do not assume
you know my story

do not take
liberties
with my ending

Not a Nice Girl

Let me always
be known
as a kind woman,
but do not mistake
me for nice.

I overdid nice.
I am hungover
from nice—
headache
still pounds.

My niceness is only
in moderation these
days—

Reserved only for
times it will not
dehydrate me

I bend over
backwards no more.
I stand upright—
firm and grounded.

Nice is agreeable,
polite—
neither serve me.

I am under no
obligation
to make you
comfortable
at the price
of my peace.

You will have
to settle for kind
if nice comes
at the expense
of my soul.

That Shit

He used to say,
You brought that shit on yourself

and this time, I
agree

As I stand
on this
impetus,
preparing
to take flight

I shake off
the goo and guts
of my transformation

I walk away,
strip naked,
leave what no longer
serves me behind:

belongings,
attachments,
feelings,
and comforts

I strip down,
let elements
beat and batter me
until I am raw

I brought that shit
on myself

my time
in the cocoon
was lonely

so much to learn
no one to teach me

That Shit (con't.)

No one could
hold my hand.

No one could
light the way.

I had to
be and feel
the aloneness.

I had to
rebuild and recreate
without attachment.

I brought that shit on
myself.

I come into my
power

I am deemed
untouchable,
scary, aggressive.

The residue
from my cocoon
still lingers.

I brought that shit
on myself.

Only those who
have spent time
in their own
cocoons are
able to stand
close
to contend
with this energy

because
just like me,

they
brought
that
shit
on
themselves.

True

and just like that
she left them
all behind
and fell
in love
with
the moon

Feral

Reborn
from fire and
chaos.

Rebuilt
from ash
and rubble.

I now only
desire peace for
my soul and
heart.

I stoke flames
of adventure
and curiosity.

When you find me, *as
I know you will*

all I ask

is to love me wild
or leave me be.

City Boy

I take him
to the woods
today. He

is mad I drag
him there.

We walk
in silence.

I give him space.

I let the magic
discover him.

I look back. He is
smiling.

A secret smile
only known to me.

He is
happy.

(Although
he would
never say
so.
His coolness
Won't allow it.)

I take
him
to the woods today
to teach him.

If he is ever
without me,
he will know
where to find me.

Then She Was He

Four days she waits for the box to arrive from Amazon. Four days she runs home and checks the mail. It is like life is on pause until that box comes. We wait for something big, but she won't tell me what. Just that she had a surprise for me. She is almost giddy with anticipation when talking about it. Her body and face vibrate with excitement. Every day after school, she runs to the pile of mail on the table. Slightly disappointed and slightly more anxious for this mystery to appear. She gives no clue, offers no ideas as to what the contents of this box will be. There is no holiday, no occasion to warrant a gift. And then, on the fifth day, it comes. I place it with the mail and look at it. I ponder the contents as I wait. The giddiness mixed with anxiety consume me now. She goes directly to the mail as she had the past four days. She tears into it and smirks. The smile is one I saw once before. At Pride Fest, when she was with her friends. A smile of contentment and completeness. Of validation. As if pulling a rabbit out of a hat, she pulls it out. A flag. Striped, pink, light blue, and white. Her eyes sparkle at its majesty. Beauty overcomes her. Without hesitation, as if she rehearsed this her whole life, she says, "Mom, I'm Leo now." And just like that, she was he. And we are still us.

Building a Boy

Where we are
is a far cry from where
we started

beautiful curls fall to
the floor

sweet little voice
deepens and cracks

shoulders broaden jaw
squares

A shot
in the thigh once a
week

in the privacy of
our tiny apartment
bathroom

he becomes him little by
little

a judge will order
his birth name dead

a surgeon will remove
parts that no longer fit

he will not be the same
person he started out as

things work
like that sometimes

he will be the person
he was meant to be

things work
like that sometimes
as well

Heir Apparent

I often wonder
what parts of me he
will keep
what little bits
will stay with him
when I am gone.

As the plane takes off,
he nudges me
with wonder
and delight.

Look out the window,
he whispers.

Sunset golden-pink,
wispy clouds muting
brightness
of hazy sky.

He smiles,
takes a picture, watches
solemnly.

In that moment,

I know.

Reflections on a Suit

We go
to three stores
can't get
right fit,
right color, right
lapels.

He knows exactly what
he wants,
exactly how it
is supposed
to look,
to feel on his
prepubescent body.

Nothing works.

We sit
on dressing room floor
together
and weep
for the suit
we can't find.

I feel the pain.
I can't make it better.
I can only sit
with it,
with him,
and feel,
cry, and ask why.

Why are we here?
Why us?
Why him?

Why can't we find
the perfect suit

to say goodbye
to his father?

Ghost

I burn candles,
light sage,
do everything I know
to remove you
from my existence

you remain
in every crack
in every crevice

you're in the corners
where dog hair collects
you're in the mold streak
on the shower ceiling

I can clean and scrub,
but you return
to haunt me
every time

I Am Alone in the Woods

and you are dying

I am surrounded
by crickets and birds,
trees and sunshine
on an empty trail

you are surrounded by
beeps and buzzes
uncomfortable chatter
from women who barely
know you.

A daughter
who is broken now

Long ago,
we had dreams
together

but now we
are not
together

We grew so far apart,
our lives don't even
intersect anymore

We were co-authors
of this story
neither of us tried
hard enough to fix
our brokenness

now you are dying,
and I am alone
in the woods

if given the chance
right now, I would
hold your hand,
remind you of who
we were before
our foundation
cracked

I Am Alone in the Woods (con't.)

I would whisper
in your ear
to remember
the love
we once shared

I never stopped
caring, I just started
loving myself
more than our
togetherness
could handle

You were
my husband
my friend my
lover

but, dear husband,
despite it all:
good, bad,
your bitterness,
my anger

the truth remains

today you are
lying there,
dying
and I am
alone
in the woods

Myth of Seven Years

I read somewhere
the human body
reconstructs itself
every seven years.

If this is true,

you never touched
this body.
My skin
my cells
have been replaced.

You never touched
this body.
You wouldn't know
this person
if she stood naked
before you.

You never touched
this body.
The tears are no
longer yours.
They run down
my cheeks
for reasons far
removed from you.

Myth of Seven Years (con't.)

You never touched
this body.
This heart
has been repaired,
sewn back
with whatever I
could bind it with.

If this myth rings
true,

you never touched
this body.

You never touched
this body.

Just Like That

And just like that

I forgive you

I wake up
I walk on
I release

the burden
of anger

that was your
parting gift

anger that had become
part of me
encasing me

falls off my body
like a blanket onto
the floor

I fold it,
put it
on a shelf

I may
need it
again

but now
the sun shines

and just like that I

forgive you

Nuclear Pasta*

You told me
I would never survive
without you

but honey,

I survived
100%
of my days
with you.

I'm indestructible.

*(Google it)

Release

At some point
along the way
I released you
I know because I am
lighter, freer

but I don't know
the exact moment

I thought it would be
cathartic
ceremonious momentous

but it just was

much as you were

I still smell
your smoke
from time
to time

but I no longer
feel it

I don't wish you ill
I don't wish you well

I don't wish you at all

you've been released

as
have I

First Marriage

blissfully happy
freshly married, I say,

*darling, we should renew
our vows in the future.*

I already married you once,

you reply.

Vows

You broke
our vows

long before
I left you.

In sickness
and in health,

you promised.

You
did
not
deliver.

You did not cheat. You
did not beat.

You did not do
anything.

You left me long
before I

left you.

Left me alone
in marriage.

Left me alone
in disease.

Left me

for your demons.

You preferred
their company

to mine.

Left me alone,
crying

in the bedroom,
thinking

I was dying.

Happy?

For a time,
I was held in captivity
cage of my own design

I grew smaller to suit
my accommodations
conformed to my surroundings

all for the sake
of peace and harmony

I squatted uncomfortably
in my cage, watching
life scutter around me

I sat in my dysfunction
and smiled

I Am a Bit Much

My scars
are long and deep
I feel a cold chill
of *what if*

I am a walking miracle
who stumbles
on her skirt hem

I am a bit much

I can be loud and take
up more space than
is allotted to me

I can be silent
and shrink
into quiet darkness

I laugh with
abandon
I cry without provocation

I am a bit much
I arrive with the weight
of several lifetimes

I sit in your space
with my heaviness

I will leave you with a
question
or an answer

sometimes both

my muchness is
overwhelming

I Am a Bit Much (con't.)

I am the truth
of the future

the pain
of the past

I reflect your fears
back to you
when the sun hits
you just so

I am a bit much

I walk into a room
demand your attention

then cower
in the corner
to avoid you

I can speak in front
of hundreds
but mumble and
stutter

to just one

I am loud
  voiceless
all at once

I am a bit much

Audacity

I sleep fearlessly

arm draped
over side
of bed

I've already met
the monsters
underneath

Chaotic Soul

I am slowly learning to
calm this spirit
of mine

she sits at the ready
anxious to fly again

forgetting she has
all she needs
surrounding her

she is scared to
sit still

she doesn't know how
to make home her
destination

Unknowingly Healed

I think
the wound
is festering
under my bandage

I left it
on far too long

I finally muster
courage
to rip it off

There, where
a gnarly gash was
is a galaxy

of beautiful freckles
begging for sun

Post Op

I awaken
from surgery
in excruciating agony

they cut me

sternum
to belly button

pulled my liver
onto my midriff

scooped out
the cancer

tucked the organ back in

coming out of anesthesia
I scream,

MY SHOULDER!

Everyone is bewildered
yet I am not surprised

I have never
been able to find
pain exactly where

I left it

This poem was selected to be published in the
2022 Lexington Poetry Month Anthology.
https://lexpomo.com

Borrowed Time (Equinox)

I sit quietly
with a cup of coffee
and my thoughts

I'm not supposed to be here
there is a team of doctors
who would confirm

I should have died
I was supposed to die

I didn't

I am very much alive

drinking coffee
with my thoughts

today is the equinox
another season

today is my birthday
another year

today just is

Diseased

Untouchable,
I am saved
by needles
taking blood

riddled with cancer
tubes administering
medicinal poison
cuffs squeeze
my arm purple

don't touch
the sick girl
she might break

I long for warm hands on
my body soft kisses

on my neck
strong arms to hold me

for you to make me feel
desirable

give me safety
from the disease
even for a second

but I scared you

I scare everyone
I scare me

if not you,
who is going to be brave
for me?

Cancer

Cancer, My Love

They pull out the needle
Throw away the tubes

I hold my breath one last
time and walk away from
you

I was cut up, sewn up,
drugged up, laid up,
and shut up
yet I walked away from
you

you took comfort
you took love
you took security
you took hope
and I walked away from
you

I turn back
for a split second

to brush the remaining
hairs from my face
and in the corner of my
eye, I see you

just a wisp of you
I catch the slightest
hint of your breath
on my cheek

I don't walk
away fast enough

there you are

I thought this dance
was over
I thought we were done

but you make it clear,

you are going
nowhere

The day after I was told I might die, a stranger gave me a cookie. A man who had never met me, except to drop trays of food on my bedside table. A man who only knew me as room 306. A man who saw me at my very worst and quietly came in and out of my room, only pausing to offer a sweet quiet smile. He gave my nurse the cookie to give to me to cheer me up. He knew I was shattered and he wanted, in some small way, to give me a little hope, maybe a smile.

The night before the cookie, I was diagnosed with Stage IV Metastatic Colon Cancer. I had just spent seven days in the hospital fighting what I thought was a liver infection. No one had ever even mentioned cancer. My infectious disease doctor was pummeling antibiotics into my system. We were going to kill the infection and my life was going to go on as normal... so I thought... so I had been led to believe.

Just a week prior it was my 45th birthday. I had gone to lunch with girlfriends. We celebrated with giant, decadent cheeseburgers at a greasy hole-in-the-wall. One of our burgers was even sandwiched between two glazed Krispy Kreme donuts. We walked out smelling like fryer grease and giggling about all the calories we had just consumed. We popped into the Goodwill next door and joked about having to size up. A fun day with girlfriends.

That evening my family took me to a local Latin fusion restaurant for dinner. The indigestion from lunch was hitting hard but I was determined to persevere and order a decadent dinner and dessert along with several margaritas. I knew what to expect, I have had gastrointestinal issues most of my life – heartburn, stomach aches, bloating, you name it. A weak constitution, I joked. But I was celebrating, it was my birthday, and I had plenty of Pepcid. I would be fine.

Spoiler alert, I wasn't fine. I was miserable all night long. Stomach cramps that would not be alleviated by heartburn medicine or Pepto Bismol. So miserable, in fact, that the next morning I called my mother and begged her to take me to the doctor. My husband had already left for work and I didn't want to bother him over a little stomach ache. Both of my parents took me to the doctor, their 45 year old baby. We went to the first urgent care center that I could confirm would take my insurance. My mother and

I went and got me checked in. Dad stayed in the car and read his book, as he did during any of Mom's errands. The wait was short; the waiting room was empty. I went back to get my vitals checked by the nurse.

My hope was they would send me home with a prescription for Phenergan for the nausea and I would spend the rest of the day in a little comfy haze, drinking ginger ale and eating saltines while watching *Oprah*. Instead, the doctor came in, took my temperature, felt my stomach, and sent me immediately for a CT Scan. I am still not sure what combination of things caused him to feel it was necessary, but he wasn't playing. He called the order in for an emergency CT and sent me packing across the shared parking lot to the imaging center. Mom following behind, we waved at my Dad in the car and updated him on the development. Both of us laughing at how weird it was to be getting a CT for indigestion, considering my weak constitution.

I checked in and was handed my creamy vanilla barium drink. "Drink half now, then the other half in 30 minutes, then we will take you back," said the nurse who sounded and looked as beige as the walls and furniture of the facility. That was by far the worst thing I have ever drank, and that is saying a lot, given what I ingested in my partying 20s.

As we waited, I started tallying up what this was going to cost me. I had a crappy insurance policy, I had to pay out of pocket for everything until I met my very high deductible. I was panicked. I was never going to be able to afford this day. This was the most expensive drink I'd ever had! I considered walking out then. A useless test for stomach cramps.

Once I was done with the drink, like magic, the tech came out to take me back for my scan. I remember the feeling when they pushed the iodine into my IV. My head tingled and a burning sensation traced down my body and settled in my nether region, making it feel like I had urinated on myself. Because why not? How could this day have gotten any worse? The tech assured me it was only a sensation, I had not peed my pants.

After the scans, I wasn't sure what to do. The doctor hadn't given me much direction but my stomach was still cramping and I was extra miserable now with the barium and dye in my system, so we trudged back over to the Urgent Care to get what I originally came for: Phenergan. I told the receptionist I wanted to speak to the doctor again about my pain. She went to get him; he came out and ushered me back to an exam room. I sat for what seemed like hours waiting for him. When he came back to the room, he started talking: "There are some areas of concern... lesions on your liver... not sure what it is... emergency room... they know you're coming... "

What he was saying was broken and garbled and I was immediately thrown into a state of shock. "... But... Phenergan...," was all I could say. I was dumbfounded.

The ride to the hospital was long and scary. I laid down in the back seat of my parents' minivan, on top of the pile of clothes they had for the dry cleaner. I cried. I had never been sent to the hospital, save the time I had my baby. What was wrong? What could it possibly be? At some point, someone, maybe me, had called my husband and let him know what was going on and that I was headed to the ER. We got there and checked in and he met me there with our nine year old.

It was six hours of uncomfortable chairs, stomach cramps, and letting my child eat from vending machines. At some point my parents took him home. And there we sat. Finally I was taken back to a gurney in an ER holding room. Vitals were taken. I was able to lay down. I begged for relief. I was cramping and hungry and scared to death. My body was shaking uncontrollably, begging for drugs and food. Tests were being run, I had to hold off on both. I was miserable.

Finally, a very kind nurse asked what my pain level was. I cried, "nine!" and she proceeded to put Dilaudid into my IV. The warm fuzz of the narcotic took over my tense body. "That's the stuff," I sighed and drifted into a blissful sleep.

My husband, concerned about work the next day, went home when I was finally admitted to an ER room. I drifted in and out through the night. I still hadn't eaten, so anytime someone would come in to check my vitals, I begged for food, shamelessly. I grabbed one woman's arm and cried "I'm so hungry." She took pity on me. She found a turkey sandwich from God knows where. It was an awful sandwich but I ate it like it was a perfectly cooked Wagyu steak.

I dozed in and out between beeps and buzzes and vitals checks. I was being admitted but they didn't have a bed. I don't remember much else about the ER visit. Dilaudid and Valium kept me in a sweet haze. I know when they did find me a bed it was on the cardiac floor. An infectious disease doctor had been assigned to me and I was started on a serious dose of antibiotics. I had an infection in my liver and they needed to find out why and how. Another CT and a liver biopsy were ordered. Holy shit. What? A biopsy... of my liver??

As I digested this not so tasty morsel of information, it was also explained to me that the infection was severe enough that I would need to go home with a PICC line and have home health administer antibiotics. A PICC LINE? A LIVER BIOPSY? How was this my life?

This was on a Saturday. They weren't sure when the biopsy guy would be in to perform the procedure. Could be today, could be Sunday, will most likely be Monday. In the meantime, I learned what a liver biopsy entailed. What it did not entail was me being sedated. A needle was going to be inserted between my ribs and into my liver while I was awake. Fan-fucking-tastic. My anxiety was through the roof. How was I going to survive all of this? When were they going to take me for the biopsy?? I asked anyone who came into my room, including the woman who cleaned it. "When?" It was all I could focus on. I had been on a steady cocktail of IV Valium. I was drifting into a nap, thinking I was safe for the day on that Sunday. When in comes a large man with a gurney. "Time to go," he said, way too happily. Fuck. Fuck. Fuck.

He wheeled me down the hall making small talk. I am not good at small talk on a good day, I am most definitely terrible at it when being wheeled down a hospital hallway on my way to a liver biopsy. When he realized this was going to be a very one sided conversation, Mr. Small Talk changed his tune, literally. He started belting out gospel tunes. Loudly, in the elevator. I was a captive audience. He prayed over me, without my consent or consult.

I was wheeled into the operating room to the tune of "How Great Thou Art." Two or three nurses were there prepping. A doctor was standing waiting for me. He explained the procedure to me. He helped me get onto the table. My right side was prepped and numbed. The doctor was friendly and told me what he was doing every step of the way. "How are you feeling?"

"I would be much better if I didn't have this needle sticking into my liver."

"Great, we are about halfway done, the nurses and I are going to have a smoke break, hang tight be right back."

"Leave the valium." As Dolly Parton said, "laughter through tears is my favorite emotion," and I was grateful for this man at this time.

All in all the procedure was painless, uncomfortable and awkward, but painless. I felt the needle go in. I felt pressure. It felt like a piece of metal sticking in my side, but it didn't hurt. I was wheeled back up by the musical gurney man and put back into my bed. A dose of Demerol for the pain and off to sleep I went.

During my stay in the hospital, I didn't see my son much. He had school and, honestly, I was a mess, I didn't want to scare him. Naturally, they brought him to see me right exactly then – high on pain meds and groggy as hell. In an emotional moment the day prior, I told my Mom that all I wanted in the world was to curl up with him and hold him. I cry as I type this because the feeling is still intense. I had been poked and prodded with needles and blood pressure cuffs. I hadn't felt the warmness of another person in a long time, just the cold nurses' hands when they changed IV needles. I was alone in a hospital bed every night, cold and shaky. I needed to hold him. To cuddle up to the life I had created. To breathe in tandem with him and smell his sweet hair. To feel the warmth and ground myself again.

What's scarier than a liver biopsy?? Being nine and visiting your mom in the hospital as she is trying to act like she is totally NOT bombed out of her gourd on Demerol. I remember opening my eyes EXTRA wide so I wouldn't look like I was sleepy or high. I think my voice went up a few octaves to give the illusion that I was being cheerful. My mother walked him in. She pulled my covers back and guided him into the bed next to me and cleared the room. He smelled of peanut butter and soap. His curly hair tickled my nose. He snuggled right up next to me and together we exhaled. For the first time since being admitted, I felt peaceful. I felt calm. I felt like I could make it. He was my reason. Still is. I needed that moment to last forever and it does in my memory. Vividly. I remember the feel of his shirt and how the blanket felt wrapped around us. When I am lost in the world or in my mind, I remember laying with my sweet boy and breathing and I am home again. We watched cartoons and I napped. It felt normal. I was feeling more hopeful about my situation.

Later that evening, we were sitting there, me in the hospital bed, my husband in the chair, he was packing up getting ready to go home for the night. Everyone else was gone. The room was dimly lit; it was close to bedtime. The TV was on low and my IV was beeping. The quiet noises had started to become a lullaby for me, making me drowsy. In a weird way, despite where I was, I was feeling comfortable and relaxed. Then the door swung open. In barged my infectious disease doctor, slightly out of breath and the nurse who had been tending to me all day, looking slightly confused.

"I've got bad news," he said, breaking my little cocoon of quiet wide open.

Dramatic pause.

Husband and I snicker. Really, it was set up like a bad joke. Like he was going to say "We're kicking you out of here, you're not sick enough," or "There's meatloaf for lunch."

A little more awkward silence then.

"You've got cancer."

And a lot of other words followed that I can't remember.

He left almost as quickly as he came. Leaving a baffled nurse in his wake, who immediately came over to us and apologized. The nurse said he was sorry for how we got the news. He was unaware of why he was asked to come in, and was just as shocked as we were. He told us how awesome my oncologist was and he would be down to talk to us soon. He told us that the infectious disease doctor who was just there actually chose my oncologist for his own son. He assured me I was in good hands. He made us promise not to Google anything.

I can't remember if I cried or sat there in stunned silence, but waiting for the oncologist seemed to take days. I was not expecting cancer. I had no family history. I had no reason to think I would ever have cancer. I quit smoking 10 years ago to the day for shit's sake. I don't DESERVE cancer. Not once while I was in the hospital did they ever even mention cancer. This was not supposed to happen to me.

At some point, the oncologist appeared. He came in the form of a sweet grandfatherly type with a mild tone and soft hands. He told me I had colon cancer and it had spread to my liver. He told me all kinds of things about treatments I would do and CHEMO. Fucking chemo.

What a word. It elicits so much when you hear it. Nausea, baldness, weakness... death.

He emphasized that it was all treatable. He talked about inserting a port in my chest to deliver chemo, he told me about the types of chemo I would receive, he gave me lists of side effects... he told me to have hope. First question out of my mouth?? Yeah, you guessed it... "Am I going to lose all my hair?" I have spent a lot of time contemplating why, when diagnosed with cancer, so many are more concerned about losing their hair and not asking what their prognosis is, not asking if they are going to die. I know why I didn't ask. I wasn't ready to know. Being told I had cancer was big and daunting enough. I couldn't even fathom the answer to that question, I wasn't ready for the answer. Hair loss, that is a question I can handle the answer to. Even if I don't like it, it still seemed manageable. There are scarves and wigs and, when I am thinking about wearing scarves and wigs... I am alive. As it turned out, for me, chemo would make my hair thin, but it didn't all fall out.

The oncologist walked out, leaving a lot of reading material and an order for a colonoscopy the next day. Then my husband left. I don't think he could handle the weight of it all. It was too much. There I was alone in a hospital room, with cancer and a gallon of colon prep... and a blown IV. I was given some Valium to calm my nerves. I'd love to say it helped. The nurse came in to change my IV. She poked and prodded, I screamed and wailed. She left in tears, unsuccessful. The head nurse came in with a vein finder, similar to a stud finder. He dug around in my arm and attempted to put the needle into several veins before he got it. I don't think it hurt really but it was something to pour my grief and sadness into. Something to blame for my internal pain. I cried and wailed like a baby getting its vaccinations. Finally, it was done. Then I had to move on to the colonoscopy prep.

It looks so unassuming, like water. It's in a big gallon jug. They gave me a straw and several cups of ice. They told me to just suck it down as fast as I could. Put the straw in the back of my throat and power through. When? Between crying jags? While I was gasping for air? It's not enough that I have cancer, but now I have to drink this venom and shit my brains out all night?? So I start... it tasted like tears and ocean water. I couldn't get it down with any sort of grace at all. It was like watching a toddler eat broccoli. I gagged and hurled all while sobbing my eyes out. I drank the ordered first half and was able to take a break from it for several hours. I put my head on the pillow, put some music on my phone and quietly digested the events of the past couple of hours. The valium did finally start to make me a little hazy... I started to drift off... but then... oh yeah... I was prepping my colon... on came the shit. All night long. When I finally stopped for a bit, it was time to drink the second half of my gallon of tears. And then more shitting... or I guess at this point, peeing out of my ass. I can't remember if I slept or not that night.

The next day is a haze. I know at some point after he got home the night I was diagnosed, my husband called my parents and told them. I know that they took me for a colonoscopy and my mother went down with me. I know that it was confirmed that I had colon cancer and the site where my tumor was located, I found out later, was tattooed. But I have very little recollection of the rest of the day. Or really for the rest of my stay in the hospital.

My mother did walk with me down to the colonoscopy. She waited in the waiting room as I was getting scoped. At that point we knew my diagnosis but she hadn't heard anyone say it yet, other than me or my husband. I think at that point she was hoping that there was some mistake. When the doctor was done, he went to give her the results. She broke into a million little pieces, she told me. There she was all alone, in a sterile hospital waiting room, being told her only daughter, the mother of her grandbabies, had cancer. My heart breaks even now still knowing she was all alone with that news. I will never forgive my husband for not being strong enough to at least go with her. Of course, I was blissfully knocked out and had no idea what was going on. And in true Mom fashion, I woke up to her put back together and ready to walk me back to my room, and walk with me through whatever was coming my way.

At some point during my stay I had a port surgically implanted into my chest. It was how the chemo would be delivered into my system. It was a smallish purple triangle with rounded edges called the PowerPort. The surgery wasn't horrible, but I was sore after; it felt like an anvil was sitting on my chest and the line that ran up my neck tugged when I laughed (the very few times I laughed).

Then I started chemo. They pumped the medicines directly into my port through my still healing skin. I had been in the hospital nine days at that point. I would be cleared to go home once it was determined my body could safely receive the chemo, without allergic reaction.

I went home the next day. I didn't have too many side effects from the first dose of chemo, and definitely no allergic reaction. I started settling into home again. When I unpacked my bags, the first thing I pulled out was the literature I had been given about the cancer I had. It was such a whirlwind of information and shock that I hadn't read or looked at any of it. Pictures of my colonoscopy, information about the chemo cocktail I would be subjected to every other week for at least a year, and a little brochure... tucked in the back of everything... titled "Late stage cancer, what to know." It included creating your will, final plans, quality of life choices... for patients with "late stage cancer." I had late stage cancer. No one had said those words to me. No one had explained how dire my situation was. Just that I was treatable and we were going to fight this. Until that exact moment, I had no idea that I had Stage IV cancer... and there was no stage V. I kept that information to myself. I was afraid to say it out loud. I kept unpacking, I tried to stuff it down into the recesses of my gut, where I stored the bad feelings I didn't want to address. What good would it be to make an issue of it? It was not going to change what was ahead. Late stage cancer, I thought to myself. Wow, I might die. It wasn't my time. I couldn't die. No one could raise my child like me. I wasn't done here yet. This wasn't how things were supposed to go. I kept unpacking, putting my hospital clothes in the laundry, my hygiene products in the bathroom.

I reached into the side pocket of my travel bag and pulled out a cellophane wrapped, institutionally made chocolate chip cookie. I was bewildered. Where was this from? It took me a second to remember the nurse giving it to me. I sat on the edge of my bed and stared at it for several minutes... "late stage cancer," I thought. I slowly pulled off the plastic and I took a small bite of the dry cookie. For a brief second, I smiled.

For the next several months, life became a whirlwind of chemo sessions, bloodwork, and visits to the oncologist. At no point in the beginning did I think that I needed to seek another opinion or question my treatment. I was in complete shock. I was just doing as I was told because I could not make big decisions or do any research; my brain couldn't digest. I was also working full time. I didn't know how to apply for disability and needed health insurance. I didn't feel like I was able to stop working; I felt pressure from home to maintain the normalcy and finances. I desperately wanted to just deal with cancer, I was a case manager for emotionally disabled youth, I really needed to only handle my own trauma, but it wasn't an option. I was grateful for a supervisor who cut me a lot of slack.

A co-worker who had a friend with colon cancer directed me to a Facebook group called Blue Hope Nation – blue being the ribbon color for the disease (not brown like I assumed). They were a group of survivors and caregivers who were in a similar boat: scared and shattered and looking for hope. It was there that I learned about my particular chemo. It was there that I learned about surgery as an option. It seemed logical, remove the cancer, cut it out completely and get it away from my body. I inquired at my next oncologist visit. He told me I was not surgical. I had too many lesions on my liver, it would be like taking a melon baller to it. I would be "Chemo for Life" as the Facebook group called it. And there was no telling how long that life would be or what quality it would have. I was defeated. Or so I thought.

In previous years my parents lived a brief while in Jacksonville, Florida, and my dad still saw doctors at the Ma https://en.wikipedia.org/wiki/Trick-or-treating yo Clinic there. My mother suggested that I hitch a ride with them for their next trip down for his checkups. Get a second opinion. What could it hurt? So, I called and set up appointments with a Colorectal Surgeon, Dr. Amit Merchea. My husband was adamantly against the idea of surgery. He had read somewhere that once air hits cancer it spreads like wildfire. I could never get him to send me that research. He would never read the research I found that showed people who had surgery had higher survival rates. "You are going to do what you are going to do," he said, and with that we agreed to disagree.

I went to the Mayo Clinic with my parents. I got scans and bloodwork and an awkward sigmoidoscopy while I was awake and watching. I spent an anxious day at the beach trying to relax with fear looming, while my results were being analyzed. Finally, I had my consult with Dr. Merchea and he went over my tests. He reviewed my progress with chemo – I had responded very well, there was steady shrinkage of tumors, and my cancer markers had gone down. "I think your best chance is surgery," he started. "I need to pull in a liver surgeon and go over this with the tumor board, but..." he continued, "I want to try. You are 45, you are young, you have kids, I want to upgrade you to chronic."

And that he did. He found a liver surgeon, Dr. Justin Burns, and together they deemed me operable. I was in the car with my family and my dear friend, Diane, on the way to her lake house when I got the call. They wanted to operate. When was I available? I decided between Halloween and Thanksgiving, I wanted to make sure I could take my kiddo trick-or-treating. Dr. Burns joked "Sure, of course, make sure you can squeeze us in." My husband didn't speak to me when we were alone for the rest of the lake trip. I was ecstatic; I knew it was my shot at life – at living.

So the day after the 2016 election, I was wheeled into a surgery room where two surgeons saved my life. They shortened my colon and ablated and resected my liver. It took eight hours. It was a very long recovery, but I survived – and here I am.

I feel like I should be rising from the ashes of cancer like some fantastic phoenix with beautiful fire colored wings spread and head held high, screaming to the heavens a song of triumph. Glorious and magnificent. Instead, it is more like I am stumbling out of a dank bar into bright sunlight after a midday bender: disoriented and confused. Forgetting exactly where I am, trying to find my bearings as the sun burns my tender eyes, I am disheveled and trying desperately to maintain composure. I don't know where to go or who to call, still quite drunk and feeling sweaty and stinky. I need sleep and a lot of water to prepare for what should be a very long hangover. I just want to find a dark corner and bury myself in blankets. I want to just sleep it off. I want to stay in the dark and let it consume me until it has washed over my body and I feel baptized in it. But I can't. This life has to go on. This post cancer, back to normal, let's pretend it never happened, life.

I don't know who I am anymore.

I have spent so much time pumping medications and poison into my body to fight the disease on the inside of me, I have forgotten about this skin I wear, these bones that carry me, the fat that sustains me. I don't know this person I have become. I feel elderly, I feel swollen, I feel like I am in a foreign vehicle that I have never driven. I have lost any connection I had with my body. Alongside all of these feelings of discombobulation I am in the middle of a horrible depressive episode. My therapist says it is all completely normal. It does not even remotely feel normal, but given my life and situation, what really does? It isn't something they tell you when you are being treated, in fact. Unless you seek out therapy, there isn't much they tell you about the emotional aspects of almost dying from cancer. No one prepares you for that side effect.

There was pre cancer me. It was pretty set. I knew who I was, what I was doing. Things were on a trajectory. It wasn't perfect but it was mine and it was hard won and had finally gotten comfortable, or so I thought at the time. Then everything turned on its head. My new cancer life came barrelling with no warning. This life centered around fighting and resting and being sick and fighting again. Blood tests, chemo, scans, more chemo, second opinions, surgery, more scans, more chemo. Do I change my diet?

Nausea, fatigue. Medical bills. Relationships strained and changed. The never-ending looks of pity and fear. Being poked and prodded, no soft, gentle touches, just needles and blood pressure cuffs. Trying to still work full time and not die. Raising my youngest, trying not to scare the living shit out of him. Trying to hold on to a threadbare marriage.

Even through the disharmony, I found a rhythm in the illness. I had one simple goal – to survive. I had a focus; I was in fighting mode. It kept me going.

Then, almost as suddenly as it came, it left. My oncologist just walked in, told me I was cancer free, and scheduled some follow up scans. He made a comment about never thinking we would get this far, laughed, and left. No ringing of a bell, no celebratory T-shirt, just me alone in the examination room, stunned. And I drove off that day with post cancer me.

After dusting off the cancer soot, I find I am no longer who I was. I just kicked Cancer's ass. This body drove the disease out. Now this body is different. My priorities have changed. I am a warrior... I am supposed to transcend all this body image shit. I am supposed to be happy to be alive and still have most of my parts. I am not. I hate my body and at the same time, I am amazed at how powerful and strong it is. I feel like a teenager again. I am breaking out and growing a beard from the steroids

I was on. My nails crack and peel. I have nerve damage in my fingers and toes called neuropathy. On good days, it's a tingle that feels like my appendages are about to fall asleep. On bad days, it feels like they are on fire. My balance is all screwed up because I can't feel where my feet are landing sometimes. I have a brain fog they call chemo brain; I lose words and have little memory glitches. People lose patience with me when waiting for me to say a word I can't recall immediately and then they just talk over me. The long, big scar that takes over my belly. And I am oh so tired all the time. I have about five eyelashes total left. "But you were lucky you didn't lose your hair," I heard too often.

Lucky... sure. Being bald is the telltale sign of a long hard cancer fight. I didn't lose all of my hair so I didn't have it THAT bad. I think even my husband felt that way. I didn't look THAT sick. It was hard for him to understand how sick I really was, which made it easier for him to dismiss my symptoms and depression. He didn't address my fear of dying or enduring a long and hard battle. He would simply say, "You're going to be fine." Because I worked and still participated in household activities, I must not have been that sick. It was business as usual at home. He cooked a few extra meals, did a few extra dishes, and thought we were all set.

I am full of angst and hatred. I can keep it together in public, but behind closed doors I cry for no reason. I want to have knock down, drag out tantrums, most times I refrain. Valium helps. I am too much of a mess to let anyone into the crazy, my family doesn't even know. I am the hottest of messes. I have visions and fantasies about throwing things and screaming and never leaving my room. Life snaps me to reality, work and kid and home all have to be maintained. If I didn't have a break from the life stuff while sick, I definitely don't get one now.

Everyone is so anxious to get back to normal. The cancer is gone, life goes on. It was a bad period but we survived and now we pick up the pieces and go on. How lovely that all sounds. Life as I knew it. For everyone else, it seems so easy. They don't have to see me weak and sick anymore. I am not wearing gloves in the air conditioning or carrying the little pouch with my portable chemo around with the needle stuck directly into my chest. No physical remembrances for those around me to remind them. Hair is going to grow back, my color will come back, the steroid puffiness will fade. Just keep on keeping on.

For me, it is a different story. It is impossible. With a high chance of recurrence, I am constantly scanned. My life is lived in the three month increments between scans. I can let go of the worry for about two and a half months of that time, but the chance of its return is a monkey on my back at all times – a constant unwelcome companion that takes up residence and with which I'm stuck living. I have a port in my chest that sticks out and every now and then I brush my hand against it and it takes me right back to the sick feeling, the complete and total fatigue. I can drive by my infusion center and get triggered. Things I love, like being barefoot, now have to be done with careful consideration because if my feet get cold, they will hurt. It is hard to have a day without cancer, even without cancer.

This sullen, angst-filled teenager longs to be deviant, get tattoos, and dye my hair. I am pubescent all over again. Moody and hormonal and depressed, nobody understands me. I am looking for my identity, the old Amy is gone. This new being is just finding herself. She is having growing pains. She is unsure and lacks any sort of confidence. Social anxiety keeps her from going out and doing things she loves. Chemo and surgery have aged her body. She feels ancient, even though she is breaking out. She cries at the drop of a hat and sometimes can't leave the bed.

Maybe I am meant to go through this period. Maybe this is my winter season where everything dies and goes dormant, waiting for spring to thaw it all and summon new life. Waiting for the sun to come and warm my tired body and the light to energize me. I told my child through this whole process that even when I was sleeping, I was fighting. When I was weak and tired, my body was readying for more. I only told him these things so as not to scare him. But maybe I should just listen to myself. Maybe I am in hibernation mode. Gathering my strength.

I know Chinese philosophy says that these times of sorrow and grief and depression need to be honored. We can't fast forward them, we must walk through them. Learn what we can and gather the knowledge we need. I am not a patient person, and I keep looking for the remote to skip this part. I want to rush through the dark time and get to the other side. I know these times are for healing and introspection, but, dammit, they are so hard. This in between time, before the rise from the ashes, no one talks about. This is where I am. In the cocoon, waiting to be a big beautiful butterfly, swimming in my own caterpillar goo.

When we were dating, we broke up once and his parting words to me were, "I just can't take the pressure, you keep pushing me to marry you. I feel smothered."

To which I was dumbfounded, because I had never actually wanted to get married, it wasn't a blip on my radar. I had never even brought it up with him. He was projecting his feelings onto me, I realized. But that idea got wedged into my brain.

I had always felt unworthy of love and here was this man mentioning marriage, obviously perplexed about his desire to marry me. We stayed broken up for about a year, then, with a dozen roses and the proclamation, "I want to marry your stupid ass," (it was funny at the time, I swear) we got back together and started to build a life. At some point I called him to the table about getting married and told him I wanted to be engaged and have a diamond ring. He told me he refused to buy diamonds because of how they were unethically mined.

I mentioned buying an antique one or another precious stone but he wouldn't have anything to do with that. I became so excited about the prospect of being engaged and getting married and a possible storybook romance that I ignored the fact that I was the only one in the story. He was just coasting along. We traveled to Amsterdam once, visited a diamond store with ethically mined diamonds... a solution! He wouldn't hear of it. He wasn't going to buy me a ring. That's when I realized it was never about the ring.

So on bended knee in the rain in downtown Lexington, he asked me to marry him. With a sweet little antique diamond ring that had sapphires on either side (birthstone for me and his daughter). A beautiful ring that I bought. A ring I gave to him to regift to me at a later day and time. A ring I saved my money for and he took credit for when presented the opportunity. My mother, years later, said she knew he was the one for me because he picked out the exact perfect ring. I fooled everyone. Made him look like a great leading man. A man who didn't deem me worthy of a few months salary and a sparkly ring.

We did a destination wedding. I was barefoot; it was on the beach in Mexico. The perfect little wedding for a non-marrying type. 20 to 30 of our closest friends and family came. His daughter, my soon to be step-daughter, was our flower girl. She was the only member of his family present. It wasn't for lack of money. His mother and sister chose not to come. The wedding was beautifully simple. A justice of the peace delivered our vows in Spanish, it was so windy the video couldn't record our voices. I had my hair curled and put up, and my dress was the most extravagant thing I had ever owned. I felt beautiful. We said "I do," with wedding rings that I bought. After we said our vows, I said vows to his daughter, promising to love her and honor her in my life. She had already been living with us full time, but I wanted to make sure she felt part of the ceremony and the marriage.

After the ceremony, a mariachi band played and appetizers were served right there on the beach. We danced and drank and laughed. His daughter cried through the entire ceremony, but we weren't ever able to discern if it was joy or sadness. Soon after she was gleefully dancing on the beach, carefree with a sausage in her hand from the appetizer table, swaying the train of my dress around to the music. There were little sausage finger stains on that dress – I adored them, never wanted to have them washed out. It was a beautiful day, a joyful day. Everyone was happy and celebrating. We had a bonfire on the beach to wrap it up.

Then he and I left for a honeymoon to a little Mexican fishing village. Our first day, I found myself floating in the pool and sobbing with my sunglasses on. What had I done? I was forever attached to this man. I was a wife! I had actually never necessarily wanted to get married. Never thought I was the "marryin' type." Then he came along and changed my mind. He truly loved me and I loved him. The tears didn't last long. I don't think they were foreshadowing anything necessarily. I was happy... just a little freaked out. We spent several days lounging and riding in boats, and resting. Just enjoying each other. Then we went home and had a marriage.

Together we started building this life, we raised his daughter and had a child together, we traveled and visited foreign countries, raised and put to rest several beloved pets, and bought a home. We did it by the book. But somewhere during the course of it all, cracks started developing in the foundation of this life we were living. We patched at first and moved on, kept living. We worked together on the big cracks and blemishes to preserve our investment. Then we started getting tired and more and more cracks developed. Patching was futile. We just started living in the mess, exposed, leaking, and damaged. We just held tight among the wreckage. Damp uncomfortableness became our lives. Eventually, we lost the will to even discuss repairs or argue about what needed to be done first.

We had these sweet reminders of the life that once was in our children. They kept us going and gave us joy. That was something we accomplished together and we did it well. They were one thing we both fully agreed on and relished. But that was a lot of pressure to put on them to be our only reason.

We were both terrible with money and whenever we talked about it, we fought. We never combined our money, always keeping things separate, so neither knew what the other was really doing financially. At first, it felt like we were smart, avoiding the argument, keeping the peace. Eventually, it was a wedge between us. Because he only saw what he was paying out, he always felt like he was paying more than me and became resentful. He would lose his shit periodically and become hostile about the unfairness. Never taking into account that I was paying for things like health insurance on both kids and made less money than him. As these resentments became more and more apparent, it was very obvious that we were not working as a team. We both felt oppressed by the other. We were sharing space and working separately on separate goals. When we tried to combine money at one point, he became infuriated that he would have to be put on "allowance." I just began to shut down and stop bringing up money all together. Cobbling together enough for my portion of the bills, couponing for groceries, shopping second hand. We both sensed things were crumbling.

Then disaster hit in the form of my cancer and it completely knocked us off our foundation. It hit fast and hard. We had no time or energy to waste on us at all. We had a task at hand and it was simply my survival. Cancer came in like a tsunami over a small island village, leaving us with the wreckage to pick up when it left. Some old, some new, all too much.

When I was sick, medical bills started piling up. Even with insurance, cancer is VERY expensive. I felt that I had to work full time through treatment, I had bills to pay. I had to keep up my end of the household. I was not given much of a break. I wanted so desperately to take time off, do chemo... rest... heal. I could have gone on disability, it is automatic for Stage IV cancer patients but I didn't have the wherewithal to figure it all out. How to apply, how to manage insurance, it was just all too much. I was barely holding on, between getting the bills paid and figuring out how to schedule my work around chemo treatments.

I prayed at night that he would tell me to stop working and heal and he would work it all out. It never happened. But I never asked out loud.

We were so disconnected that at one point during my treatment, while I was swimming in medical debt, collectors calling me frequently, he had paid his car off, leaving him with an additional $300 a month, so he bought new musical equipment and paid to press a CD of his band's music, while I prayed I could one day get out of debt. We weren't equal in this partnership. We weren't lifting each other up anymore. We were just co-existing.

Even later, while he was dying, he made sure I couldn't have any financial ease. He created a living will and trust that appointed his sister the executor of his life insurance and retirement and didn't allow either child access to their money until they are 28, unless they went through her, ensuring that I would never benefit. Never mind I would be left raising our child alone and I had already raised his child, providing for her financially and emotionally almost all of her life.

I survived cancer, seemingly, WE survived cancer. We went back to our uncomfortable co-existing, taking up the same space but not connected. Funny thing about cancer is that it strips you down to nothing. Chemo breaks your body and your spirit. When cancer is done, you are left in the ashes of your own destruction. You have to rebuild but you don't have all of the parts and pieces you started with. You have to gather what tools and support are there and they are oftentimes unfamiliar and uncomfortable. Life doesn't look like it used to. Suddenly, things are prioritized. Extraneous and irrelevant do not get the time and attention anymore. My soul started to crave all things authentic and meaningful and our marriage was not that. I started to realize my worth and seek things bigger than he could provide. You rebuild and you change because who you were doesn't suit this new life anymore. I couldn't even pretend to be a part of that old life anymore.

Throughout our marriage I begged him to see a doctor. He was overweight, smoked, and didn't exercise. He was not a healthy man. He needed to be checked. I had Stage IV cancer, one of us needed to survive for these kids. Even after all we went through with my colon cancer, he wouldn't get a colonoscopy... he said the one doctor he liked wasn't in practice anymore. And that was that. Wouldn't look for a new one. I sent lists of doctors in his network, I begged him to get screenings and physicals. He didn't. I eventually gave up. I could only worry about my own health and pray he wouldn't die at home with my child there.

Soon after I recovered from cancer, he thought he was having a heart attack early one morning and went to the hospital. He ended up being diagnosed with GERD (acid reflux). He came home from the hospital at 10:30 AM on a weekday with a large bag of salt and vinegar chips. As he sat there on the couch with a soda and chips telling me had GERD, I asked if the doctor informed him that diet was a factor and pointed at his snack. "I don't need you to tell me!" he yelled, and that was the last time I brought up doctors or his health. From that moment on, I just planned for him to die. He was obviously slowly trying to kill himself. This was when I began to really consider leaving my marriage. One of my parting statements was, "I fought like hell to live and you are busy trying to die."

My... our marriage wasn't all horrible. We had some beautiful moments. It is hard to bring them to the light of day because the end was so contentious. We loved our kids. We would sit at night and talk about what good jobs we were doing. He had to work past an undesirable childhood to become a decent father. He worked hard at it. We had backyard parties and joyful times. But life has taught me that two truths can co-exist: a husband can be a good father, someone the community loved and respected, and he can also be a bad and neglectful husband.

I will be unpacking my marriage the rest of my life. I have healed. I have moved on. I have dated other men. But 20 years of gaslighting and being made to feel unworthy takes some time and therapy to process. Parts of me wish I had left him sooner. But I know to my core I left at the exact right time. I stayed for my kids. I stayed because I was afraid I wouldn't make it without him. I didn't realize I had been making it without him all along. I left when the pain of staying was far worse than the fear of leaving. Before I left, on a rare date night, we had a discussion about one of our dogs. I had told him how the dog tended to me while I was sick, staying by my side, sleeping right next to me, giving me comfort. He instantly become irriated with me and snapped, "I took care of you too! I don't know why the dog gets credit. At least I didn't leave you." Which I think sums it all up.

Forgiveness came in an unexpected way when I was least prepared. I had harbored so much anger it grew comfortable and expected, it was just part of me. I knew how to operate enraged. I was functioning on sheer spite and getting things done, but forgiveness slapped me right in the face and left me shocked and speechless for quite some time. Processing it and allowing it to become part of my journey has been oddly easy and surprisingly difficult all at once.

I remember the first time I met her, his mother. We had dinner planned at a local, upscale Japanese restaurant, a place I had been wanting to try for a long time but could most definitely not afford. I wore dark jeans and a black v-neck sweater with a silver beaded necklace as an accent. I wanted to impress her but not look too overdone. His sister was also included in this dinner, as at most get togethers she was Mama's side kick and backup. The restaurant was predominantly done in neutral tones with black accents. Sparsely decorated, some plants thrown about for color. We sat at a table for four in the middle of the restaurant, servers and guests swishing by constantly... I ordered conservatively... a simple udon dish. I didn't want her to think I was in it for the fancy free meal. I only drank the wine from the bottle that had been ordered for the table. I loved her son, I wanted her to love me. I was so nervous and intimidated; she had such a presence and was so serious. Conversation was slightly uneasy though not unusual for a first meeting.

At this point in our lives, my not yet husband had just begun to take over full care of his daughter, her mother admitting that she was unable to meet her needs and signing over primary custody to him not long before this meeting. He was so very proud of the father he had become and he was so dedicated. He worked very hard at erasing the mistakes of his upbringing and offered her the unconditional love he felt was never given to him. Together we had committed to putting her first, even though our relationship was just beginning. Was it perfect? No. Was it based in love? Yes. As our vegetable tempura appetizer was being served, the tension started to surface. She almost immediately began to berate him for the things he was lacking in as a father. As if she had a checklist, one by one, she checked off her talking points. He was not hard enough on her about school. He didn't discipline her properly, he was too soft. We spoiled her too much. The hits just kept coming. She didn't ease up at all. The dinner ended in me crying in the bathroom, feeling hated and like I was failing this child I was trying so hard to help raise, and him storming out of the restaurant to smoke a cigarette. I had never had anyone talk to me so horribly about something I was trying so hard to be good at. Raising a child who wasn't mine, loving her through her pain, and my confusion as a guardian with no experience. Now looking back at the scenario from a different lens, I also see the theme of him leaving me alone to fend for myself when things got hard, but that wasn't something I was even close to realizing at that point in time. After the check was paid and uncomfortable goodbyes were taken care of, he and I headed to the nearest bar to debrief. It was then we agreed that anytime we went to dinner with his mother, we ordered well and drank a lot.

I remember the exact moment when I started to forgive, that I could feel the anger lift from my heart a little. I was sitting in my therapist's nondescript office in the middle of a cluster of surgeon's offices on the third floor of a medical complex. Again with the neutral tones. She was probably about 10 years younger than me. I liked her youth and validating, empowering style of therapy, it was sometimes like having coffee with a friend. She was able to nonchalantly pull out little truths and revelations from me without it taking much effort or many tears on my end.

Sitting in an office supply store chair under an office supply store painting, I would offer up my concerns, feelings, and jumbled thoughts. I always sat with my coat covering my lap, making myself cozy. She joked that my mental health was dependent on my coziness and she was so very right, I am an open book when I am comfy. I was recounting my married life for the two thousandth time and remembering yet another instance when I felt oppressed or neglected. Processing my marriage and its demise has been an ongoing ordeal that I am not sure I will ever come to the end of, though it feels like it has tapered off through time.

Memories do still come, instances flood in and they sit on me, it is hard to send them on sometimes. It's difficult to come to terms and move on when you can't argue it out or get closure. With him gone, there are only my memories and they are one-sided. I know I am not the hero in every story, but I have no counterpoint. I have no one to give me the other perspective, no one with whom I can duke it out. He deserves to have his story told as well but it is not my place to do that.

I was rambling on, complaining... processing... trying to make sense of whatever incident I was working through. My therapist stopped me mid-sentence, crossed her legs, and leaned in toward me, her blonde hair falling off her shoulders, glasses perched on the end of her nose. "You've worked in mental health, you know a little bit. If you had to diagnose him right here, right now, what would be your best, most educated guess?"

When talking with friends and family, I had always contended he had chronic depression, still do. It got worse and worse over the years. He closed off more and more. But in that moment, at that particular time, I said something I had never considered: "Attachment Disorder."

We both paused and were taken aback by the words that came out of my mouth. She was almost speechless initially, then she simply said "Huh, yeah." It was almost like an involuntary muscle twitch, I didn't seem to have control of my mouth, it just came out. It was like it had been stored in the recesses of my brain but never processed or considered, specifically waiting for this opportunity. Then it just shot out. It all made sense. All of a sudden, things were clearer, I had a better understanding.

I am in no way qualified to diagnose anyone, nor did he ever consent to being diagnosed in his lifetime, to be very clear. But I had worked with several clients when I was in the mental health field who had attachment disorders, and, though it hadn't dawned on me until that very minute, it fit him like an old, well-worn shoe, based on my very limited experience. Looking back at what I knew and saw, his attachments to his family seemed strained, at best. When he recounted his childhood, there were never happy moments or warm memories. Sometimes it was like the more traumatizing it was, the more attached to the memory he felt. At dinners with his family, they recounted the Christmas his mother withheld all of the presents with great fondness. He frequently told the story about walking alone at a very young age on the Interstate to try to get to his father, like other people recount their birthday parties and reunions.

I remember one Thanksgiving dinner with his mother, his sister, and our little family. His mother started making a weird gagging noise in the middle of the usual political discourse that came with dinner at their table. She kept on making the noise, the weird gagging, until we became concerned that she was having an asthma attack. Then all of a sudden, she started hysterically, maniacally laughing. Confused, his sister asked, "What's wrong,

Mama?" His mother began to recount an instance in my husband's toddlerhood when he had a febrile seizure. The gagging sound she was making was to imitate the sound he made while in the middle of said seizure. As she told the story, she kept laughing. I have never been more disturbed or confused in my life. So much so, I hesitate to even tell this story at all because it triggers a feeling of deep pity and heartache for him. And it is almost unbelievable as a mother to me. What would have been my scariest moment in parenthood was a source of comedy at the dinner table for her.

More of my memories go back to the time we would take the kids over to see her at her large, perfectly furnished, yet stark and chilled house when she lived in the same city. My son was just a toddler, barely walking. He loved to be held, he still nursed. I would cuddle and hold him any chance I got, knowing my time with him like this was limited. My husband's mother would get visibly upset with me. "You are spoiling that baby." "Let that baby cry." I brushed it off. I didn't really think much about it back then. We had inherent differences in the way we mothered. I knew what my baby needed and spoiling him with love and affection was how I chose to mother. Holding him when he cried and rocking him to sleep was the only thing I knew. In her eyes, making them strong meant letting them cry it out, preparing them for the cold, hard world. It was as though she normalized feelings of pain and distress and made them co-exist with love and support for him. To be a child raised like this it is hard to distinguish healthy, good feelings of love from feelings of panic and hurt. I wanted to be my child's safe place. She wanted to be a lesson.

As I processed all that we had been through, that HE had been through, I came to a place of pity and sympathy and it felt much better than the anger I grew so accustomed to. Did she ever hug him or comfort him when he was sad? Not that I had ever seen or he ever said. Did she lay in bed with him when he felt scared and make him feel like he was safe? I have no way of knowing for sure, but all evidence points to no. And how very awful for a child to not feel safe and loved. In the adult relationship between mother and son, there lacked any intimacy, hugs were rare and always awkward. He tried so hard to make her proud in the things he said and did but she never told him she was proud. After he visited her, he would be agitated and seemingly depressed, it was never a "feel good" experience to have dinner with his mother.

I think back to the birthday parties I had for the kids. My family always had celebrations for our birthdays when we were children. It didn't matter how much money we had, we always had cake and friends and joy for our birthdays.

My mom made invitations out of construction paper for me to take to school and hand out. I was always made to feel so very special. They are wonderful memories that I always wanted to have for my children. We never had a lot of money, he and I, but I always had a fun party for the kids, usually with a theme. In the process of planning these parties, I would have to deal with his criticism and disdain. It was too much, we were spoiling them, not worth the mess, he would always complain. Many times he didn't participate, sometimes he stuck around and complained the entire time. If I planned the parties at a place that had a bar, like a pizza joint or bowling alley, he tolerated.

One birthday, in particular, he blew the fuck up. It was my son's messy party. We let the kids finger and body paint, dig through jello, eat messy things with their hands. They had a blast, it was in the back yard so we could hose everyone down after. It was all too much for him. Off to the side of the house, he had a meltdown. I was spoiling my son, it was a huge mess. In his defense, I usually planned these things without consultation. Ask forgiveness not permission was a tactic I took with my husband for most instances. He was not prepared for the chaos and mess going on in his safe space, his back porch. In the argument that ensued, I yelled at him, "Did you ever have a birthday party as a child, can you not remember the joy of it??" He simply said, "No," and stormed out of the house. He took off for several hours. Once everyone had left and things were settling, he came back and I had a revelation: he was jealous of our children. He never got that unbridled joy of being celebrated and adored. His jealousy made him feel shameful and guilty. As we continued with our lives, I started paying close attention to that anger when it presented itself. That anger, when provoked by his shame and guilt, was most often directed at me. I am, by nature, nonconfrontational. I hate an argument or any sort of conflict and avoid them whenever possible. When he was reactive with me, I simply shut down. I stopped engaging and waited until it all blew over. I planned my routine to have minimal contact, rather than addressing, discussing, and moving on.

In our relationship, his treatment of me, especially when I was sick, was seemingly neglectful. He didn't know what to do or how to comfort me. It was almost as if he was afraid to make me too soft to fight, if that makes any sense. It was hurtful and isolating. There were times I just wanted him to sit with me and hold my hand. To tell me I was brave and strong. His way of comforting me was to say, "You'll be fine, you know you will." It was a lot like times in our marriage when I needed a little ego boost and asked if I looked nice and he would get frustrated and he would tell me, "You know you're pretty, why do I have to say it?" It was not what a partner does. A partner uplifts their significant other, makes them feel good. It is love, it is support. They keep trying until they get it right. He was never shown love that way, though. How could I expect him to understand and show it to me?

Now that I have words to put to the way he treated me, I can be in a place of forgiveness. Now that I have the gift of perspective and hindsight, I can release anger and hatred. He was afraid to spoil someone he loved. He didn't understand that you can't love someone too much. In this place of forgiveness, I can see how hard it must have been for him to be the father he was. How hard he must have tried to keep the connection and bond he had with the kids. How he had to teach himself to be affectionate with them and probably go against all he knew to do it. How awful it must have felt to be jealous of your own child's happiness. Detaching was his default. He fought his instinct for our kids, and for that I am forever grateful. What a gift he gave them, the gift of a happy childhood.

I thought forgiveness was going to be some big sage burning, letter writing, ceremonial, cathartic breakdown thing, but it has been quite the opposite. It has been a slow and steady meditation. Memories that lead to revelations, quiet discoveries in the middle of the night in that little sweet time between awakeness and falling asleep. A moment when you are open and ready to receive. When your conscience is unarmed and new thoughts and ideas can waltz in for consideration. No big crying jags, just simple understanding. Forgiveness and sympathy have not meant that I was deserving of the neglect and judgment, however. Forgiveness simply means I have opened up my heart and my soul enough to see beyond my own pain. To see the pain he had so deep within him, pain he was unable to acknowledge or confront for reasons only he knew.

My forgiveness sits next to my anger, calming it when it threatens to rage. Forgiveness offers me a softness in my being and in my heart, that allows me to continue on and be open to love again. Part of me is sad to see my anger tempered. I drew some power from that aggression and hostility. It carried me through some hard times that could have broken me otherwise. But, in retrospect, it was not healthy nor conducive to living a life of contentment. It was holding me back from true happiness. Sometimes, all that being said, I do allow the anger to emerge. It has a place. It deserves space and it helps me get shit done.

This part of my story is my most important. To some this will seem like an attempt to explain myself, to make people understand. For me, these events... the period of time I am now writing about... are what led to important realizations about life. How, if I was to live a life of joy and quality, I had to let go. Let go of the perception of myself that I held close. The person who many loved and respected. The kind and sweet mom who took care of everyone, and to some the greedy and bitter almost ex-wife. I had to let go of concern for other people's perception of me. To stop worrying what everyone thought and the idea of me they carried in their own minds. To survive this life, we have to stand on our own laurels and do what we need to do and hope we hurt no one in the process... but casualties sometimes happen.

We had been texting for a few days. I wanted to talk. I knew he didn't have much time left. I wanted to talk about the future of our children. How did he want his legacy to carry on? What stories did he want me to make sure they knew? There is a gift in knowing someone is dying – you can prepare, you can finish things. I also wanted to discuss the retirement and life insurance money he had and how it would best support his children. That was my agenda. We agreed on a Monday. I would stop by and we could talk.

I went to the house, the house we created together as a family, the house I left so I could find my happiness. I knew his time was coming near. I knew he was dying. When I arrived, he was sitting up in bed. In the room that used to be ours. In the room I used to sleep in, the one I thought I was going to die in. He had taken any memory of me out of it. It was bare, the bed he was in was tall enough that not one bit of his six foot six inch self could touch the carpet when he sat over the side. He was gaunt, he looked so weak. His face looked as though it was melting. His dreadlocks just spilled out of his head like vines in the jungle. He wouldn't look up when I came into the room, he wouldn't look at me. I was scared of him. I was scared of the way he looked, the confused, breathless way he was talking, and that he was going to die right then and there. Over 20 years together came down to this – this poignant and important small period of time. I froze. I was full of fear. How do you wrap up so much in one little moment? How do you make things ok? Come to a conclusion?

"I have some things upstairs I need to grab," I said.

That's how you do it, that's how you face death... you divert and run away. I forever wish I had done that differently.

I packed up some things I had left in the house and loaded them into my car. I wiped a counter, moved a chair, I did everything possible to not have to go back in that room for a while. I didn't want to face him. He was mad and bitter, he was dying, he wasn't the man I knew anymore. How would I talk about these things with him? How would we work this out?

I finally mustered up what little courage I had and went into the room. He appeared to be sliding out of the bed, he was breathing heavily. He sat there half on, half off the giant bed, hand rested on his knee. I offered to help him back into the bed, silently hoping he'd decline. I was afraid to touch him. He refused. He still wouldn't look up at me. He had refused any help I had offered since he was diagnosed. When he found out he was very sick, I offered to come stay with him and help take care of him. Of course he refused. He was too proud.

In that moment, I wish I had forced him to look at me, to talk to me. I let his anger and bitterness loom over the room like burnt grease lingers in a house for weeks. It just sat on us both. I didn't know what to say. I had made a list. I had put to memory all the things we needed to work out. I knew that this was going to be our very last conversation. I knew I would not have another chance.

He had not talked to our 11-year-old son about his prognosis at all. All our son knew was that his dad had cancer. Nothing more. He saw me fight it and come through to the other side, so that is what he expected. A bad year with Dad feeling like shit, then crawling back out again and back to life. Our boy had no idea it was this bleak. Early on in his diagnosis, he emphatically insisted that it was his business to tell his child. He never got around to it.

"I'm not sure what to tell him," he said after he knew it was terminal.

I wanted to scream! You tell him you're dying, you tell him you love him and you will be in his heart forever. You write a letter, you give him sage words of wisdom. You fucking DO SOMETHING. He deserves a last conversation for shit's sake. He is going to be blindsided, it isn't fair. This was cowardly.

"I will handle it now," I said. "I have an appointment with Hospice in a few days, I will consult with them and go by their suggestions. You put it off too long, it is out of your hands and on me now."

"Ok," was all he had to say.

At this there was silence. I was silently stewing, I had been left alone with the task of telling a child his father is dying. Why hadn't he talked to him???? I was once again stuck doing everything myself. Even in death, he is ducking out of the hard stuff. Lucky him. Rather than continue with the conversation and make sure I covered all my points and questions, I let anger and resentment creep in. Not much else got accomplished.

I asked about his life insurance and retirement. He got defensive.

"It's taken care of. The kids split it."

He drifted off. He came back. He seemed confused and asked what we had been talking about. We had so much we needed to say to each other but it had become too late. We should have talked, we should have listened. He wasn't the man I married. Hell, he wasn't even the man from three weeks ago. Disease had taken over.

I knew as I left that whatever I said upon exit would be my last words to him. "I have always loved you. I will always care," I said, mostly meaning it.

And I walked out.

I got nothing accomplished, nothing was taken care of. I had put it off too long. I was scared and uncomfortable and the moment was gone.

Two days later, he was admitted to the hospital and didn't go home again.

I am unclear on why or how exactly his quick downfall happened. Reports from his friends say that he had fallen and was unable to walk and had to be carried, all six foot six inches of him, to the car and into the hospital. I have heard he was belligerent and tried to rip out IV tubes and get out of bed. I heard he was incoherent and unable to determine who was in the room. I heard he thrashed and moaned for periods. All of my accounts of this time are from third parties as I was not allowed access to him. I only know my side. I can only tell my story.

I received a call at some point from his sister when he had been checked into the hospital and I was to remove any of my remaining belongings from the house, if I did not, they would be put onto the street. She offered to rent storage but my items were to be removed in two days either way. I told her that my things were all upstairs in a loft area and that none were in his way, should he be coming home. I offered to clear the couch from the living room should they want to put a hospital bed in there. The house was still in my name, I was still paying half the mortgage. We had filed for divorce and soon after he was diagnosed, I didn't feel he should go through a divorce while sick, especially after finding out he was terminal.

My stalling of the divorce was read by my in-laws as a tactic to get all of his money so they began the process of making sure I had no benefit from his death. Never mind I supported him through layoffs and low pay, raised a child who wasn't mine, would be tasked with raising our child together without a father, and had spent over 20 years with this man. They were set on getting the house for whatever reason. If it was that simple, I would have given it to them. I left him and the house, I didn't want the house back. But I knew, since we didn't divorce, I would end up with it. I was never sure if this demand to remove my things was a tactic to take possession or power over me or both. I called a lawyer friend, who called a judge, who made sure there was an order stating they were not to remove anything from the house without my permission. And so began the saga of anger and animosity between his mother and sister and me. From that point, I would not allow them to speak to me directly. Only text or email and, eventually, only through a lawyer. They say grief is sometimes disguised as anger and these women were ANGRY. I was their target. I am sure I still am.

It was Wednesday, and I was preparing my son for his first summer camp experience. Ironically, it was a camp for children affected by cancer. Because of my cancer, initially. He was so excited for his first overnight camp. We were shopping for camp gear and packing. Now his father was in the hospital. What do I do? Our adult daughter was tasked with being the middleman for his mother and sister and me. No one would speak directly so we left her to do the talking for us all. Not a role a 22-year-old losing her father should have to play. She had the task of relaying to me that I was not welcome at the hospital. She also relayed that it was expected that our son would visit. She also indicated that she and her grandmother and aunt were trying to figure out the best way to tell my son his father was dying. I firmly told her to let them know that it was no longer in anyone's hands but mine. It was too late for him or anyone else to have the conversation. Our son needed to hear this from the only parent he will know going forward. Not women he barely knew. We had an appointment on Friday with Hospice, so I would consult with them on the best way to talk to my son.

On Thursday, I checked in with our oldest. She said they were trying to get him to eat and get his energy up. If they were able to do that, then our son should visit. Through the day, I was given no updates on his condition. I know friends were visiting. It seemed unfair to have them report to me what was going on. I spent 20 years with this man. I was being denied access to even the most basic information, yet told over and over that everyone expected my child to visit. I was not going to send my son into a situation that I had no way to prepare him for and I most certainly wasn't going to let him go without me. Since the Hospice appointment was scheduled for the next day, I chose to lay low and wait for the grief counselor's advice.

We made it to our scheduled appointment with Hospice, my son still not knowing his father was dying. We had been living with my parents during the separation so he hadn't noticed his dad's absence. Over this time, my son saw his dad change dramatically, from a big, strong man to being gaunt and frail, and it made him scared to be with Dad. This man wasn't the father my son knew. Alternatively, he wasn't the father he wanted to be for our son. I knew the man... he never would have wanted his son to see him fade away. He most definitely wouldn't have wanted our boy to see him in the hospital with no control of his faculties.

The Hospice counselor was a colleague from a previous job. We weren't friends, but we had familiarity; it was comforting. She called us back to her office but I requested to speak to her first. My son thought we were there because both of his parents had cancer, but I needed to talk to her about our situation. I told her his father was in the hospital. I asked her how I should tell him his father was about to die. I asked her if he should visit his father. I asked her if he should go to the overnight camp he was so excited about and leaving for the next day. She sat with me and helped me plan. Helped me get perspective. Helped me figure out how to tell my son his father was dying, he was about to be a fatherless child. She helped me mother my son because I was at a loss.

The camp he was supposed to go to, Camp Kesem, is a camp for children who have been affected by cancer. He had been packing and planning for weeks. He had never been to an overnight camp, and he was beyond thrilled. The freedom of a kid who didn't have to contend with his parents or their issues for a whole week was there for his taking. The counselor and I discussed it – what if he went and regretted it? What if he didn't go see his father in the hospital? What if he stayed home and waited for his dad to die with the rest of us? What if he saw his dad, barely conscious and struggling to breathe?

She gave me a tissue and calmly told me that it was his choice. He needs to know all of the facts. His dad is dying. His dad will die very soon. His dad is in the hospital and won't be going home. His dad may or may not know he was there. His dad in that bed isn't the big, strong dad who he knew. His dad loves him very much. Then he chooses, camp, visiting in the hospital, saying goodbye...

all his choice. "But what if he regrets his choice?" I asked. "Oh, he will," she answered. "Whatever he chooses, he will one day regret. He is in a lose/lose situation, so he should have some autonomy now." Because grief isn't linear, it doesn't work on a timeline, he will grieve the death of his father his entire life. He will be mad, he will be unbearably sad, and he will regret – it is unavoidable. We spent an hour processing, *How am I to do this in the best possible way?*

It wasn't fair to him to break the news in an office with a stranger, so he never joined us. Honestly, I was hoping she would just do it for me. It was the hardest thing I could ever imagine doing. I knew this already because I thought I might die once and I had planned how I would tell him then. How I would write letters and give him sentimental things so he would know his mother as he grew up. I was so mad at his father for not being brave enough to say goodbye. For not giving him the chance to hug him or tell him he loved him one last time. To just leave things hanging. I wish I had been brave enough to facilitate that.

We went to my parents' house. I brought him to the screened in back porch where I liked to spend my time there. It was just the two of us. I sat him on the wicker couch and hugged him. I gathered myself and took a deep breath and explained to him that his father was dying.

I can't remember my exact words. I can only remember curling up together on that couch and crying. Holding my soon-to-be-fatherless boy and wanting to take away the pain. He had been through enough, why him? My mother came out and put a blanket around us. We just held onto each other and slowed our breathing to match each other's much like that night in the hospital. I gathered myself and told him that if he wished to see his father, he could, I would take him. The past several weeks were scary, he had watched his father shrivel away, lose his words, and fall in the shower. He had been avoiding him already. I told him that whatever choice he made was the right one and that I would stand by it forever. We talked about his camp, that his father would most likely die while he was there. I know I told him that his father loved him very much. He paused and thought for a bit. I asked if he had questions. He didn't. He simply said, "I want to go to camp."

"Ok," I said, "let's get you packed." As we packed him up, I made sure that at any time prior to leaving he could see his dad, I would take him. He didn't want to. It was scary, I understood. We talked about all the ways his dad influenced his life and the good times they had. We went about our day, planning the drive to camp for the next day. We discussed what would happen when his father did pass. I contacted the camp and let them know.

I double checked if he wanted to go say goodbye. We recorded a message for his father to listen to telling him how much he loved him. At points during this time, I would get messages from my daughter telling me to bring my son to the hospital but never any information about his condition. I finally explained that Hospice recommended letting it be his choice and he chose not to go.

The next day I drove him to the camp about an hour away. He was so excited but so afraid to be too excited. We checked in, we took his things to his bunk. He met his counselors. We both knew he wouldn't be there long; he was trying to soak in every bit before he would leave. I said goodbye as he was running off with a new camp mate. I cried the entire way home.

On Monday I received a text from a mutual friend of ours. She and her husband had been at the hospital by his side much of this time period, for which I am grateful. They had been concerned with me being able to go see him at the hospital, but I had already said goodbye. This time was for his daughter and family. He didn't want me there, I was sure. But our insistent friends felt it was best, I didn't have the wherewithal to say no. They determined that this was the time, that I should go see him. It was nearing the end and his family was amenable to my presence. I drove over, on autopilot. I saw a few of his friends at the hospital entrance, I followed them to his room. There he was. The big, strong, proud man I had known most of my adult life was almost done with his journey. His dreadlocks were bunched up above his head; his breathing had become more shallow and slow. His daughter sat next to him, holding his hand and talking to him, playing music he loved. His mother sat in a chair in the corner, tear stained and broken. His sister sat near her, on high alert watching his every breath. A few friends were in the tiny room as well. There I stood. It was awkward and uncomfortable. I most definitely wouldn't get time alone with him. There was a noticeable tension in the air. I wasn't welcome, I was tolerated. I stood over our daughter and just sent him well wishes for his transition through silent prayer. I looked at him, closed my eyes, and begged the universe to let him transition peacefully. The man lying there wasn't my husband or the father of my children. It was his shell, that man was already gone. He was not lucid or coherent. Had I been allowed time alone, I would have told him that I would make sure his son knew all about him. I would keep his memory alive. I would thank him for the good times we had. It wasn't all bad.

Very soon after my arrival, his breathing became even more labored and his sister became distressed. She called the nurse and cleared the room. I was grateful; I didn't want to be there anymore than they wanted me there. I went home and slept for hours. I knew it was almost time. I had no energy left.

That evening I received a call from his mother, he had passed. He was gone. I was numb.

The next day, I called the camp. I let them know I would be picking up my son but let him have all of the fun he possibly could before I got there. My mother drove me, I couldn't do it alone. It was the perfect summer day, clouds were billowy, slight breeze. The ride was silent. When we arrived, the director met us at the entrance. She sent a counselor to go get him from the activity he was involved in. We stood there, waiting. Trying to hold it together.

He came over the hill, his giddy grin disappeared from his face the minute he saw me. He knew. He paused. Almost as if he was thinking about running the other way. Once he got to me, his father would be gone. He was free until he had to hear the words. Part of me hoped he would run, I didn't want to say the words. He walked slowly across the patch of grass that separated us. I moved toward him. When we finally got close, he fell into my arms and we both crumbled to the ground. I don't remember my exact words. I just remember wishing I could have let him just have the rest of this week to be joyful and free. I was going to have to drive him home, find him a suit, take him to his father's service, and then raise this fatherless child.

We were gently ushered to the nurse's cabin to talk and gather ourselves. We went to his cabin to gather his things. It was messy and smelly and perfectly exactly what a boys' summer camp cabin should be. Guitar propped up on the wall, wet socks and swim trunks hanging all over, yesterday's already forgotten craft project shoved in the corner. It was a scene of pure joy and I had to remove him from it and take him to utter sorrow.

Soon after we got back home, we had to buy a suit for the services. He was very specific about the sort of suit he wanted. He had a vision. It was the suit he would say goodbye to his father in, I was going to honor that vision as best we could. We started at Target. Nothing fit his stocky, short frame correctly. Nothing was quite right. Grief takes many forms; this day, it took the form of complete frustration and disappointment. He lost his shit right there in the middle of the men's underwear section. It wasn't about the suit, but the suit was somehow going to make it better. I wasn't about to argue and I was ready to spend whatever amount of money was necessary to make this one thing go right. We found a few second rate options. We went to the dressing room. Both of us knew none of them were right, we knew before we went into the stall. But we also knew we needed to find a spot away from the bright lights and summer shoppers. So I hung the jackets and pants up, pulled my boy down onto the bench with me and held him tight and gave him space to let it out. There in the Target dressing room. The same Target dressing room that I snuck away to when he was a baby to sit and nurse him in the middle of a shopping trip. We held tight and cried together. We cried until we were done. We shopped until we found the perfect suit three stores later and went home.

We weren't involved in the services. I am not even sure my husband was. It was at a local funeral home. It was brief and impersonal. It was to go from 2-4 PM on a Sunday but it was over and the crowd was cleared out by 3:30. His sister and friends spoke. A few moments before it started I was asked if I wanted to say anything. I hadn't been given the option until that very moment, just as the music started. Almost as if by offering it could be said that, "After all that time together she couldn't even say something nice at his funeral." I would have, I had a lot to say. He was the father of my children, we spent over 20 years together, but I couldn't wing that, not on the spot.

After the service I was asked to sign his cremation orders. The only involvement I had been given in any of this. The only time his mother even looked my way. My dear friend Jennifer, who is also a lawyer, grabbed my arm and asked if I felt she should be present. I didn't. I signed them. I know, out of all of this, that was the one thing he would have wanted.

After the funeral service, there was a gathering at his favorite bar. All of his friends and fans showed up. It was packed, a party he would have loved. They played his music and toasted his life, people were spilling out the door. It was grand. A proper send off, his style.

I overheard rumblings, because drunk people aren't as quiet as they think they are, "She won't get the house." "I hope she doesn't think that house is hers." I wanted to scream... of course I would get the house. I was on the deed, I paid mortgage on it up until he died. It was my damn house. And it was the one thing I DIDN'T want. I walked away from that house of despair and disease and depression. I most certainly didn't want it back, but it became my inheritance, ironically.

In the end, I am sorry to say he died angry and bitter. With the help of his mother and sister, he changed all of his retirement accounts to ensure I did not benefit in any way from his inheritance. Despite the fact I would be left with his child to raise alone, and I had already raised his daughter. He turned control of the estate to his sister and ensured the kids would not have access to their money without his sister's permission until they were 28. He was so mad at me. His pride was that hurt. He spent more time signing these documents than say goodbye to his own child. His family acted like I was in it for the money. Like I hadn't spend all my time and energy and resources raising these kids, and like I wasn't going to keep doing that regardless. I cried to my therapist that I felt like the black widow. Though I most certainly did not kill him, I was being treated as if I did. My very wise therapist pointedly said one day, "Then own it. If you feel like the black widow, then own it." "Huh?" She explained that you can't change or control how others perceive you. You can only keep on living and doing the best you can. How others feel about me is of no concern to me. If I am the black widow then so be it.

107

We stood together in our tiny bathroom of our tiny apartment, giggling nervously as he prepped his needle. We probably used 12 alcohol swabs, a gazillion disinfectant wipes, and washed our hands seven times each. Partially because we were afraid of contaminating the area, and partly because we were stalling... at least I was. It was finally the day. We had been waiting for the prescription to arrive at the pharmacy for almost two weeks. Covid and some red tape held everything up. I was glad – please don't ever tell him. I just needed more time... to prepare, I guess. Some days our life just seemed so huge already and adding anything else to it felt even harder. The day was so big... yet so miniscule and mundane at the same time. And so it was, my 13 year old son injected his first round of testosterone into his leg. By himself, while I stood watching.

I tell my part of his story with permission. I write about it because this may be a substantial moment one day for someone else and maybe they will feel a little less alone. I am processing my feelings by putting them to paper, out and away from him because he does not deserve nor does he need to witness them; he only needs love and support from me. He has seen me break; he has seen me at my most broken and vulnerable. Not now, not for this, for this he needed his warrior mama, the one who is right behind him taking up whatever arms are necessary, holding the bandage and celebrating the beginning of the rest of his life with chocolate cake decorated with a rainbow flag.

My heart stopped when that needle went into his leg. I had my chemo port removed from my chest while I was still awake and, yet, this seemed more painful. He paused, then drew the testosterone into the needle, took a deep breath, paused again, then hastily handed the loaded needle to me. "You do it," he said, then he quickly took it back. "I have to do it for myself," he said, took a breath, held it, and jabbed it into his thigh.

Our little world halted. Silence. It felt like it took me several hours to take a complete breath again. He is the bravest person I know. He is my guide on how to live this life.

I am not sad, I have never been sad about this, about him. He hadn't been my little girl for a long time. By second grade he was dressing and presenting as a boy. I have a picture that I ordered from the school in his last year of grade school. It was all of his class pictures lined up. They progress from girly-girl to boy easily and effortlessly, curly long hair, getting shorter and shorter, frilly dress morphed into dress shirt. He has lived his life with no explanation or apology since birth. His sense of self has always been the strongest and most assured I've ever known. He has eased me into his transition almost like it was intentional and planned.

When he was born, I vowed to just let him be who he was. I never pushed gendered toys or clothes on him. For a long while, he was happy with long hair and pink clothes. Told everyone his favorite color was hot pink, like Dora the Explorer. He twirled in flowy skirts and wore princess shoes, we were victims of the persistent glitter plague that attacks many families of female identifying children. One year, for Christmas, he asked for a dump truck and a Barbie in red. Slowly, he began favoring "boy" clothes and wearing blue and red. We always talked about colors being for everyone so I was glad to see him genuinely finding things he liked and not sticking to expectations or norms. He picked from the boys department whenever we went to the store. Honestly, I was happy; the clothes were better quality, sturdier, and fit better. We went to the "girls" department for only one thing: underwear. Part of me knew the day was coming and that was the part of me that still held out just a little bit that this was a phase. I enjoyed buying the unicorn and rainbow panties; they spoke to my inner child. Part of him being a little girl fed my inner little girl; I was able to do and buy the things I always wanted or loved when I was young. It felt good. One day, my mother had taken him to a department store and I got a call, "Umm, she said she wants boys underwear."

I was taken aback. It seemed so weird. Why? This was it – this was the moment. He wasn't my little girl anymore. I sat there, his whole childhood flashing before me. Swirls of pink and glitter and pigtails were running through my heart. She was becoming he and, while I was perfectly fine with it, I was still a bit floored.

Mom was still on the line, "Amy, what do I do??"

"Buy him some, I guess," was my respsonse. Why not? It was then, with his dinosaur boxer briefs, that I started to see this might not be the tomboy phase we all thought. Underwear was a statement, a declaration. A finality. We were on a new path now.

The only thing, other than pink underwear, that caused me to mourn was the name. It was so hard to stop calling him by his deadname. His father and I agreed on very little, but that name, we picked it together. It had meaning; it was chosen specifically for a sweet baby growing inside me. I sang and talked to her in the dark of night – we had a secret special bond. I loved that name. My heart still skips a little when I hear it. I had to find my own private ways to say goodbye to it. I didn't want him to ever feel that I felt like I was missing out on another life, one where he wasn't him. I sat outside with a candle one evening and spoke that name to the wind. I said goodbye, I sent my little girl off with all of the love that my heart had in it. I told her how much I appreciated her part in our journey. She was the dream come true that I didn't know I wished for. I cried for her, not because I missed her but because I was so grateful to have known her and been her mother. Her free spirit and unabashed confidence got us this far, now her job was done, time to move on.

There were times we would go to events and people would mistake my kiddo for a boy. I would correct their pronouns. I would explain to strangers, "That is my daughter, she just dresses like a boy but she is, in fact a girl."

Then one day, I looked over as I was giving my schpiel to the man ringing up my kettle corn order at a festival and saw a look in my child's eyes that said, just stop. I quickly thanked the man and walked over to my kid.

"You don't want me to correct people, do you?"

"Mom, they're strangers, it doesn't matter what they think."

"Does it bother you that people call you a boy?"

He simply said "Nope."

And with that we just stopped worrying about it and making a fuss. It was then that we just lived our lives without regard to pronouns. Because at that time they all fit.

To say I am not scared is just not true. I am raising a black transgender boy. The world hasn't been historically kind to them. We often have talks about safety and being aware of his surroundings. Compliance with authority if it means coming home alive. We see the news, trans kids dying in uneven proportions just for being them. I am scared because my experiences and relationships with men have been subpar, at best. I am working through my issues, but what have I... what will I project onto him? I am scared because I worry that I am not enough for him. Does he need a man around when things go sideways? How do you raise a man? Men in our lives, save for my father, since our series of unfortunate events, have all but vanished. Do men stick around? My therapist says yes but

I have yet to see that. How do I raise a man who stays around? How do I raise a man without a father? I know I am quite a bit on my own, how will my too-muchness affect him? These are all rhetorical questions. Questions I ask myself in my weak and vulnerable moments. I do not need anyone to assure me or volunteer to help. I have managed and will continue to manage with as much grace as I can muster. I am preparing to watch my son enter a second adolescence and become the person he is meant to be. It is raw and emotional and scary as fuck. It is also beautiful and poetic. An adventure for only us two. But we have everything we need to make it work and come out even better than we went in.

I don't cry often. It's rare for me to cry in public, it feels performative when I do. But when it comes to him, I cry. I cried a little when he came home with those underpants, when I hear his deadname. And I cried right after he put the first of many bandages over his needle mark. I held him too tight, too long and he let me. I told him he was the bravest person I knew. I told him how proud I was of him for living in his truth no matter how hard. I told him I looked up to him. He cries whenever I cry. So there we stood in that tiny bathroom for a very long time crying together. I have been crying pretty regularly ever since. Not always out of fear, there are tears of joy as well. If you could see him pose in the mirror when he is feeling fully himself or hear him sing with unabashed joy in the shower, you would know that he was meant to be this person. And I was meant to be his mother. This is a step toward him being his complete and happy self. The decision to start testosterone was an easy one in that regard.

I also cry whenever I send him into the world without me. Whenever he is away from my protective bubble, the community I have created to keep us safe, I cry. How will they treat him? Today, coincidentally, was a day I sent him into the world. I signed him up for an event that was geared toward boys of single mothers. He is a boy. I am a single mother. The event organizer knew we were coming and that he is trans. He assured me that all would be fine. Yet, I dropped him and saw him stand by himself looking a little lost and I cried. I called a friend who would see them at the event breakfast and asked her to keep an eye on him. Called my mom for consolation. Then I pulled over and just cried. I am not scared of much anymore but I am scared for him. All the time.

So here we are, he and I, ready to start yet another adventure. I get to watch him grow into the young man he was meant to be. I get to watch him become a complete human being and live his very best life. I am proud to be his mom. I am lucky and grateful that the universe blessed me with him. This life is everything because he is in it. I know this is the right path because it feels right because he is joy personified. Because he is happy. Because he looks in a mirror and can see the person he is supposed to be. I started a quiet and subtle gratitude practice with him when he was just a baby. I point out our blessings and talk with him about how wonderful our life is in moments of calmness.

I say to him often, "What a great life we have created."

To which he typically responds. "THE BEST, Mom."

I will raise this young man to the best of my abilities. I will fuck up, I will beg forgiveness, then I will pay for his therapy.

Four years ago, March 18, 2018 at 1:12am, I ended my marriage. I know the exact time because I was looking at my phone as I walked into the house after coming home from an evening with friends. I know the time because I was hoping he was already asleep. He wasn't. He was sitting on the edge of our faded, sunken, worn out sofa drinking a beer, waiting for me. The same sofa he had been sleeping on (by choice) for years. He wanted to talk. I wanted to go to bed. He wanted to discuss our marriage. I wanted to end it.

We were together for over 20 years. We had children. We had a life we created. But there were cracks in our foundation that were no longer fixable. At least, not from my perspective. Things hadn't been good for a long time. We were ships passing in the night. We were both to blame for that. I no longer wanted to try. He apparently did. He said he felt I had given up on our marriage. I had. Honestly, I didn't even think he liked me at this point in our lives. I told him that, and he sat there in utter shock. Not many more words were exchanged. I was done, there was no fight in me. I simply stated over and over,"It is broken and I don't want to fix it."

I had discussed leaving him with my therapist. I told her I wanted to separate, she asked if I had intention of working things out. I didn't. She told me it wasn't fair to let him think there was a chance if there wasn't. We rehearsed what I would say. We talked about sticking to the reason and not going down rabbit holes of blame. At this point there was no blame, it was simply over. In my mind and heart, there was nothing left, nothing to fix.

At 8:38am the next morning, I left our marriage and our home for good. I left with a bag. I walked away from that life. I had slept one last time in the bed in our room. The bed I nursed our baby in, the bed I slept off chemo treatments in, the bed I slept alone in for more years than I would like to admit. I walked out of the bedroom, through the living room. He watched me, we said nothing. I went to my parents'. There are many details to fill in about that night and about us. Our relationship had been over two decades long, we had a complex story. This is not that story. This is about four years.

A lot has happened in four years. Those who know my story, know that he was diagnosed with cancer soon after I left and he died within a matter of months. Those months are their own story. This is not it. This is about four years.

For a number of months after I left, my son and I had no home of our own. We used guest rooms, stayed with my parents, and house sat. In that time I began the scary, daunting business of preparing to become a single parent. We began divorce proceedings and not only did he fail to provide any support for our child in that transition, he was gearing up to fight any request for support once the divorce was final. His pride was hurt and I needed to suffer no matter who or what might be collateral damage. My son visited him occasionally, when his work would allow, and he passed soon after. We rented space in a friend's home. Then, finally, we were able to move into our own place. We found a tiny apartment at the end of a complex that backed up to a field and creek. I had never even considered an apartment complex before. But this was our new life. The one we were rebuilding from scratch. I needed us to be uncomplicated and safe and this seemed like the best option. In these four years, we have created a home. Our house, the one I left, had stopped feeling like home for a long time. I spent a lot of time away from that house to avoid the dark cloud within. I involved my son and myself in anything that would fill our schedule and keep us away. Now, our home is peace. Home is my art collection. Home is where I light candles and burn incense and play my music. Home is where my boy sings in the shower and binge watches *Drag Race*. Home is the two of us, Tuki the dog, and Lula the cat. Home is where we all breathe.

In these four years I have been single. Unattached, unpartnered. I have dated. I have learned so much about myself as a woman. I have reflected on who I am as a partner. I have learned my worth and my strength. I have learned where I need to improve for my own good. I have learned my traumas, even childhood ones I didn't know existed. I was very lonely in my marriage, but the loneliness of being single is a welcome change to me. I have learned that I have support and when the loneliness creeps in, I need to reach out and access it. Loneliness is a sign or symptom of something more than being alone. I need to look within. I now know that people, even a partner of 20 years, cannot read minds and that sometimes you have to tell them how to take care of you. You can not fault them for not knowing how. You can fault them for not trying, however. I now know how to advocate for myself. I know to be vigilant about having my needs met and that it's ok for people to think I am an asshole in the process. My worth is not determined by anyone but myself. No one's attention or love is more important than the love I give myself.

I have only recently been able to say I was abused out loud. Saying so feels so weak and unempowered, not the person I am now. But it is my truth. I was not beaten or verbally thrashed, rather I was neglected and deprived of affection, attention, and finances. I was made to feel worthless. It has been hard to marry the fact that he loved me and abused me. That those two things can be true at the same time. It is even harder because he didn't do it intentionally. He was only able to love in the way he was loved. Had it been purposeful, it would have made more sense, been easier to understand. He was a well known and well respected man in the community. An admired musician, people wanted to be in his presence, but he wasn't the same person to me. Mutual friends turned their backs on me, unable to believe this and unwilling to validate my experience. For a time, I felt like a terrible person. I left a man, he died. Bad timing, but it looked so suspicious to an outsider. I kept in mind what my therapist said about the black widow, "You have no control over what people think of you. You can spend your life trying to make them feel better about you or you can spend your life feeling better."

In this time, I have waded through financial hardships I thought I would never survive. He made more money than I did, it was one of the reasons I stayed; and though I paid more than half of the bills and groceries, I thought I needed him financially. All alone, I have provided for us, I have made all of our ends meet, and scrounged enough for extras, like trips and adventures. I have surprised even myself by being just fine on my own.

I know I have the capacity to love again. To maybe one day even partner again. That, even though I am still healing, I am able to let someone in. I can open my heart and am worthy of healthy, authentic, and unconditional love. My therapist has had to constantly remind me of what normal relationships look like. A man I dated went shopping with me once and actually seemed to enjoy it. I was giddy. My therapist had to explain to me that it was normal for couples to shop together and do mundane things and not hate it. And that my bar was set WAY too low if that was what I was excited about. I know that if I do partner again, it will be with someone I WANT in my life and not someone I NEED. Someone who I choose and keep choosing, that it will be worth the work it will take. I am learning to communicate and to talk about my feelings, no matter how silly it feels or how awkward it sounds. Years of having your feelings ignored and invalidated makes it hard to trust what is going on inside your head. I remind myself daily that my feelings are valid and real. I don't hide them or run from them anymore. I know how trauma feels in my body. I know when I feel anxious I need to move and be outside. When I am sad for no reason, I need to write. I know that years without affection or attention have left me on a constant search for dopamine rushes and I have to be careful. I also have to watch myself with dating apps, social media, and alcohol. I want to feel good to the detriment of all of my other emotions.

Four years have gone by so quickly. I am on the other side of so much. I am a different person. I am a different mother. I am happier than I ever thought possible. I am grounded and stable. I am home, wherever I live. I am grateful and fortunate. I am surrounded by love. I have found a voice as a writer and poet. I have found myself.

As I write this, there is a cat purring on my lap, a dog sprawled across my bed snoring, and a child singing quietly when he should be sleeping in his room. In our previous home, a television was on constantly, serving as a reality buffer and distraction. Now I don't watch TV much anymore at night because the sounds of my life are so much more satisfying.

ABOUT THE AUTHOR

Amy Figgs was born in Ocean City, Maryland, spent her youth in various Pennsylvania towns, and landed as an angsty teen in Lexington, Kentucky. She began blogging and writing poetry as a way to process trauma and grief and found a small audience online. With the encouragement of lovely friends and family, she pulled together her debut collection of essays and poetry: *Upgraded To Chronic*. When she is not writing or working her day job, you can find her wandering through nature or enjoying time with her son and friends. Her status remains "No Evidence of Disease."

CPSIA information can be obtained
at www.ICGtesting.com
Printed in the USA
BVHW020538230123
656853BV00005B/14